WALKOUT

ARTHUR L. BROWN

DESEGREGATION

INTEGRATION

SEPTEMBER 23, 24, 25, 1969

Publisher's Name: Arthur L. Brown

ISBN: 978-1-968442-46-0

Table of Contents

DEDICATION

I would like to dedicate this book to all of the students that ever attended T.L. Weston Jr/Sr High School. All of the teachers and parents that worked together to ensure that the African American students received the best education possible. Also recognizing all of the citizens of Greenville, Mississippi.

Special recognition to all of the students that attended T.L. Weston September 23, 24, and 25, in 1969. All of you that assembled together to ensure positive changes were made. Changes that relate to the inequalities in Mississippi's unfair treatments of African American students. Your bravery will always be remembered in this book.

Last but not least, the men and women at the Delta Ministry. These people were the true leaders in Greenville's struggle for civil rights. Their courage to take on the establishment during the struggles for equality in Mississippi will always be remembered. "To God be the Glory."

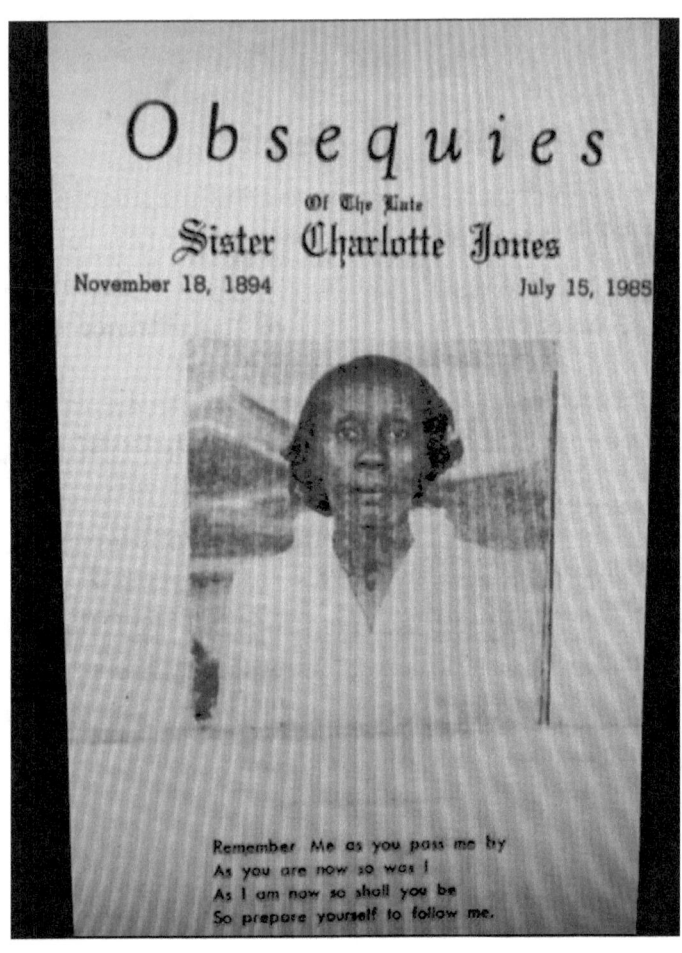

Obsequies

Of The Late

Sister Charlotte Jones

November 18, 1894   July 15, 1985

Remember Me as you pass me by
As you are now so was I
As I am now so shall you be
So prepare yourself to follow me.

INTRODUCTION

In the early 1960s, the Greenville, Mississippi public school system was segregated. The white schools were well-equipped and well-funded, receiving updated supplies and equipment, while the black schools were ill-equipped and forced to share books and other used equipment that was handed down from local white public schools. There also were discrepancies when it came to the food that was served in the cafeteria and other resources.

On September 23, 1969, the students of T.L. Weston Junior/ Senior High School staged a walkout in Greenville, Mississippi that helped bring awareness to the ongoing problems within the school system. The students presented a list of demands to the Greenville public school administrators and the local school board. (Delta Democrat Times 9/23/1969) p1

It was only after threats to boycott the local businesses that consideration was given to the demands presented by the students that attended T L. Weston. By sharing this information and bringing attention to the struggle students faced in the early 60s, we can inspire and motivate present and future generations on the importance of a quality education. After the civil rights movement in the early 60s, Mississippi was still segregated for the most part. The state refused to integrate; therefore, black communities were left behind when it came to economics and education.

Nearly all of the public schools were underfunded, and the disparities between white and black schools was unbelievable. Many of the students that attended the black schools, along with the teachers, felt that there were very low expectations and low standards for education.

The local businesses were predominately all white-owned. Most of the jobs that blacks could get were well below minimum wage, and several black parents struggled to keep stable housing and food on the tables for their families.

The majority of the jobs that blacks held consisted of very hard labor and long work hours. Black women had to work outside of the home to help support the household. They had to work in white homes cleaning, cooking, and taking care of white children.

Times were very hard for black families in Mississippi, and with all of the hardships, young blacks began to open their eyes, looking forward to a better tomorrow. Young black men took on a stance of wanting to create a better life, refusing to continue in the same directions as their parents. They decided that an education was the key to opening up opportunities to create a better life for themselves.

The federal government had mandated that Mississippi, along with other southern states comply with the Civil Rights Act of 1964. Mississippi was one of the few states that refused to agree with the change.

Groups of African American children began to band together to strategize to create a culture of change. Starting with the school system, they staged a protest against the school board of education and administrators. In the past, the voices of black teachers were not being heard, but once the students became involved in trying to create a change in the education practices in Greenville, Mississippi, teachers became an active part, joining in the protests.

The first high school for blacks in Greenville, Mississippi opened in 1920, it was named Coleman High School, after Lizzie W. Coleman. She was principal of the district's segregated no. 2 elementary school on Theobald Street for more than forty years. Like many black Mississippi teachers and educators "back in the day," Lizzie Coleman had no college training. Forced integration would bring destruction to the legacy of this great high school.

When Coleman became a Jr. High School, all of the memories—trophies, pictures, and awards that represented decades of great accomplishments— were thrown away into garbage dumpsters with no respect.

Greenville caught the attention of the Coleman Report researchers in 1965, when its school board defied Mississippi segregationist Governor Paul B. Johnson Jr. and the obstructionist White Citizens' Councils to submit its own freedom of choice plan to the US Department of Education. The 1964 Civil Rights Act Commission chose Coleman as the school in which they would study the state of school inequality across the United States. Greenville, as a result of this move, became the anonymous city to be the model for Coleman's integration plans. (The Nation 10/13/2016) p1

CHAPTER ONE

CONDITIONS IN THE AFRICAN AMERICAN COMMUNITIES IN GREENVILLE

Allow me to begin this story by reflecting on life in this African American community. Years before the protest at T.L. Weston Junior and Senior High School there were many issues that had negative effects relating to poverty and hardships within the city limits of Greenville, Mississippi and all around the Mississippi Delta. Blacks were the least educated people throughout the state. Many adults in black communities could barely read or write their names. There were only a few public schools in the Mississippi Delta for black people.

The schools African Americans attended were years behind in academics. The academic materials provided to teachers were outdated. Considering that it takes at least ten years to update books for the classroom, most of the materials used in preparing the students to be successful in school were outdated by almost twenty years. The students had to use books and other resource materials that were handed down from the white schools. During this era, school buses were not available to take students to and from school. Therefore, no matter where the students lived, they had to walk to school. Parents that were fortunate enough to own and drive a car would drive their children to schools. In spite of the many challenges and setbacks, the students met them head-on. Mississippi's State Legislature was spending three times more on white students by the 1950s than on black students. In the mid-60s, the teachers were well-trained and dedicated, ensuring that the students received the best education possible under the circumstances.

In Greenville during this time, there was only one high school for black students, so the students that lived on the south side of town had to walk to the other side of town to attend school. Most of them had to walk four to six miles every day. Located on the northeast side of Greenville, Coleman Junior/Senior High School was the only high school within the city limits where African American students attended.

There were three elementary schools on the north side of Greenville: Julia L. Armstrong, McBride, and Weddington. On the south side of Greenville, there was only one elementary school: Lucy L. Webb. All of the elementary schools were first grade through sixth grade. Back then, many of the students that were old enough to work went to work in the cotton fields and at other domestic jobs. Children would miss school because of the need to help their parents pay the bills. Southern states depended on common labor to harvest their cotton crop. At this time period, cotton was the primary crop, and younger children were allowed to work in the fields when they couldn't get other jobs. It would not be long after the mid-60s when this rule would change. Before the changing of the age rule, in rural areas, students could attend schools as long as the cotton and other crops were not ready to be harvested. This rule applied to the families that lived on the land owned by the farmers. In some cases, school-age children had to miss more than a year from school.

Many would not attend school regularly so that they could take care of their younger siblings while the parents worked. Because of the high number of days missed from school to provide support to the family, a number of students were behind in their grades. Therefore, several students were much older than their classmates. Age limit was not a real factor, and understanding the circumstances and conditions, administrators made exceptions for students to play sports no matter the age difference. Allowing the students to continue to play sports was not only occurring in Greenville but also statewide and in neighboring states.

In the rural areas, students attended O'Bannon Junior/Senior High School. O'Bannon school was located southeast of Greenville outside of the city limits. These students were bused to school. Back then, rural area churches were used for school, and many of them could only hold a few children due to lack of space.

Inside the city limits of Greenville, many African American students attended school regularly. Their parents knew that their children needed an education, and they wanted a better future for their children. Many parents had jobs in which they had to work long hours for very little pay. They knew that education was critical to establishing a better life for their children. Most parents had little or no academic training, but they understood the value of having at least a high school diploma.

With only one elementary school on the south side of the city, there were too many children piled up in those small classrooms, and each teacher had a class full of students. However, the teachers took their jobs very seriously and were loyal to their professions. A few years later, because of the overcrowded classrooms, students that lived north of Central Street would ride the bus to Weddington Elementary School.

Children that attended Lucy L. Webb had to walk to school every day. Sometimes while passing through the white neighborhoods, they were harassed by some of the white people that lived in the neighborhoods, so the students would walk in groups to and from school to feel secure and protected. Parents or older siblings would often walk with the children, especially the younger ones.

Not all of the white people that lived in the area were mean-spirited; some were friendly, and on weekends, white boys and black boys would occasionally play sports together. There was an open field at the base of the levee next to the Corps of Engineers building where boys of both races would meet up. There were times when the boys would mix up to play sports, which included football, baseball, and basketball. There was a closeness among the people from these neighborhoods, and some of them would come to watch the young boys play sports. The workers at the Corps of Engineers building would also come out to watch the young boys play.

The boys were highly skilled, and they played the games very well. Some of the boys later got the chance to play sports in college, and a few got the opportunity to play professional sports. This story is one of the most talked about in the neighborhood.

The south side of Greenville had a mystical sense about it. For the most part, people seemed to get along very well. Of course, there were some children that were bad apples, but everyone knew who they were. In some neighborhoods, the men and boys would gather to kill hogs during the winter months to keep food on the table for the family. Afterward, they would divide the meat so that every family could get a good portion. They would hunt deer, rabbits, and squirrels. In the spring and summer months, people would go fishing in the many lakes surrounding Greenville. There were several fruit trees in some neighborhoods. In the spring, some of the elders would plant vegetable gardens, including tomatoes, okra, peas, corn, squash, beans peppers, watermelons, and sweet potatoes.

The girls stayed close to their mothers and other women to learn different skills. The women taught the girls sewing, cooking, and housekeeping, as well as taking care of their hair. Some of the girls were very good at sports and would play softball and basketball with the boys, and some excelled in track and field.

When boys were interested in courting girls, they had to go to the girls' parents to ask for permission to see the girls. When visiting the girls at their homes, the boys were closely watched, especially by grandparents that lived in the homes. Some girls had older brothers that were highly protective of their sisters.

This high standard of morality was expected among families at that time. Young people were taught to respect one another and to respect their elders. Most of all, children had to go to church to learn about God, Jesus, and the Holy Spirit. Young people in most families had to attend Sunday school—no exceptions.

In many households, the church was first. There were many churches in Greenville. On Sunday mornings, the African American people were scattered about, holding church in their own buildings throughout the city. These practices of division between black churches can have negative results and should teach us that people that pray together stay together.

In the early 60s, the Greenville school board leaders proposed that students could choose among any of the district's sixteen schools. This was called freedom of choice. Only a small group of 147 black students—one-tenth of those eligible—decided to enroll in the all- white schools. No white students crossed over to attend the all-black Coleman High School or any other black elementary schools.

The black students that volunteered to attend the white schools were not welcome at their new locations. Racism fueled the hate that white students had for blacks, and they practiced harsh treatment toward the black students. The white teachers also contributed to the injustice that many of the black students had to suffer. The black students would share with their parents and others about the way they were treated. Still, some of the students were treated fairly, as there were some decent whites in Greenville. When the African American students were provided the first opportunity to attend white schools in Greenville, the events that ensued were daily news in the black communities.

These courageous young black students were the first to break the barriers of segregation in Greenville, Mississippi. They were trying to get the best education possible. Their parents knew that it would not be easy for their children. Some of these young people were from black families that had decent incomes. Some of their parents were doctors, teachers, business owners, lawyers, and government workers. In time, due to the difficulties that the black students had to endure, some of the parents removed their children from those schools.

Weston Students Halt Morning Classes

CHAPTER TWO

THE BUILDING OF TWO SCHOOLS: A NEW START

In the fall of 1964, two new schools opened on the south side of Greenville due to over crowdedness in many of the existing schools. Solomon Jr. High was built on the southeast of the city, and T. L. Weston Junior/Senior High School on the southwest side. Also, many of the people from the rural areas were moving into the city limits. Greenville was expanding with a growing population, which forced the city limits to be expanded.

When Solomon opened its doors, it was predominantly white. The white students that had attended E. E. Bass Jr. High no longer had to cross town to get to school. Now, they could stay on the south end and go to Solomon. After leaving junior high school, students from both Solomon and Bass would attend Greenville High School. Greenville High, along with St. Joseph, were the high schools white students in the city attended.

T.L. Weston was the second high school in the city African Americans could attend. Since Weston was built on the south end of the city, students no longer had to walk across town to get to Coleman. When the school first open its doors, children from sixth to eleventh grade would start their new journey.

With the opening of T. L. Weston Junior/Senior High came many mixed feelings. Students coming from Coleman High School had to leave a school that held many memories for them. A school that several of them had become attached to. But change had come. It was time to forge a different direction yet making the transition from Coleman to T. L. Weston was not going to be easy. At Coleman, some of these students had excelled in many areas. The elementary students were looking forward to joining their older brothers and sisters that attended Coleman, but instead, students graduating from Lucy L. Webb elementary school had to attend the new south side school. At first, having the two high schools in Greenville for blacks created some division with the students on the south and north sides. Realizing this change and the different directions they would follow, the students took it all in stride. The older students that moved from Coleman High School to T. L. Weston had to take the lead in helping the younger students transition into high school. Their leadership was important and provided an opportunity for the younger children to have role models in many areas of life. Sports was the area in which experienced kids really helped the young ones get grounded.

The older students from Coleman were leaving a school that had a great tradition.

Coleman was well known for great football, baseball, and basketball teams, as well as track and field. Many of the students that played sports at Coleman were fantastic athletes that went on to have great college and professional careers. The Coleman Band was well known throughout the state, and the band director was one of the best in the state. The Coleman High School Choir was rated one of the best in the country. The choir director was known nationally. She later became an Icon in music and well respected by many professionals in her field.

The older students that came from Coleman had many challenges ahead of them. They had to start a new chapter not only for themselves but also for the younger students that depended on them to set the standards for academics and sports. Many of the older students brought great skills with them. They were the pioneers that lead the way for a better tomorrow.

After the transition of students from Coleman to T. L. Weston, teachers also came along, and they had to adjust to the change as well. Some of the teachers that had to move from Coleman were nearing retirement and had experienced a fulfilling career, looking to retire from this outstanding school. The younger teachers, some just finishing college, made the transition with ease. However, they all came ready to do their jobs, facing new changes and challenges. T.

L. Weston was a new building with many updates that didn't exist in other schools. The ultra-modern school building had a front entrance with glass panels. The entire school was fully air conditioned. The library was in the center of the building, with sunken steps where one had to step down to enter. The glass panels of the library walls created a beautiful view as one walked by, and the well-lit room allowed a beautiful ambiance. Doors were located on each side, allowing easy access so that students didn't have to walk around the library to enter. The library was staffed with a librarian who was a retired military soldier, a very strict disciplinarian that implemented the rules of the school and took no mess from anyone. When students entered the library, the quiet and orderly environment required them to have a focus.

The first year at T.L. Weston was challenging for most of the students. The school's sixth graders were the first of their academic level known to have the experience of attending a high school at such a young age. The teachers kept close check on them. The seventh graders, however, seemed just fine. They were eager to mix it up with upperclassmen. Some of the seventh-grade boys joined the football team, where they competed with the older, more experienced boys. Several others joined the band. Due to the small size of the band, seventh graders had the opportunity to march soon after joining. The band director was a young man with great skills and a very good music teacher. He received his early training from Coleman High School's band director. The seventh graders were a highly motivated group of young people. They had graduated from Lucy L. Webb the year before attending Weston. Mr. Weston retired the year before the six graders graduated elementary school. The teachers saw that this seventh-grade class had great potential. In this grade, there were many A and A+ students. Before their journey was over, this class would do many great things.

The eight graders came from Coleman. They were cool kids, and they would reference the classes under them as little children. Many of them were very good students and athletes. From day one, they were rivals with the seventh graders. Both classes were eager to attend the new school. Only one year separated most of them in age.

The fact that the south-end students were in the same building created a natural bond. There were brothers and sisters attending the same school. Sometimes that would present problems, but usually, the older siblings were very protective of their younger brothers and sisters. As time passed, they all would become like family. That was a testament to how children were raised "back in the day."

The students that lived close to the levee had to pass through part of the white neighborhood, but there was rarely trouble. The white people in that neighborhood were very friendly most of the time. They were the ones that played sports with the young blacks. For the most part, racism was not so out front in Greenville in those days, but it did exist. However, African American schools still operated on a much lower budget than the white schools. That problem never changed, even after the opening of the new school.

T.L. students had old, handed-down books and old equipment from Bass and Greenville High. The food in the cafeteria was not so good, so some kids brought their own lunch to school.

Although Weston was a new school, supplies and equipment were not always available. The teachers would often complain about the lack of supplies, which they needed to do their jobs. The handed- down equipment from the white schools were not enough. These problems were due to lack of proper funding for the black public schools. The state of Mississippi was notorious for a lack of equal distribution of funds and materials for African American public schools.

However, the teachers were determined to do the best job they could. They would often buy supplies for their classrooms with their own money. The students were taught to work hard and make due to learn under all types of conditions. The teachers would say, "We made it to college, and so can you. Hard work will pay off, just keep trying." In addition, the parents were supporting the teachers. The parents and teachers were teammates, and the students knew that they could not get away with foolishness at school. In spite of the lack of funding, the teachers held the students to very high standards.

Requests for equal opportunity between the white and black public schools were overlooked by the State School Board of Education, although the state constitution called for separate but equal public school systems. This problem would be the defining moment that would enforce integration not only in Mississippi but across the entire country. America was divided when it came to race, equality, and justice. Many problems still exist today.

Sports played a big part in the early days at T.L. Weston. Weston soon became a school that competed with the best. From the start, the athletes from Coleman were well known. Some of them had set records in all areas of high school sports; they were considered stars early on. Weston was off to a pretty good start. These boys and girls had competed on the big stage in high school sports at Coleman High School as the Big Eight State Champions.

At the start of the football season, the team was trying to find its identity. The team had very good players, even though the new students on the team were playing high school sports for the first time. The next year, the school joined the Little Six Conference and lost only one game.

The basketball team had great success from the very start. The girls' team had some very good players and very little competition.

The baseball team was very good also, as were the track and field teams. Some of the upperclassmen were already record holders. The boys' 4x100 relay team set the state record, which lasted for many years. Later, the girls' 4x100 relay team would set the state record, also lasting several years.

The Junior/Senior high school offered industrial arts for grades seven through nine. Home economics was also taught on the junior high school levels, but these courses were always underfunded. Often, the supplies and equipment needed to properly teach the students were hardly sufficient; however, the instructors did the best they could to ensure that the students got all that they had to offer. This was also the norm for the music and science departments. The vocational center was located on Raceway Road, northeast of the city. There, students could learn skills like automobile mechanics, brick masonry, sheet metal works, and welding. Students from both Weston and Coleman attended these classes and rode the buses together.

No matter how difficult the challenge, the teachers would not give up on accomplishing their goal, which was to teach their students. In that era, teachers were committed to their profession. Education was golden in the African American communities, and being a teacher had a certain prestige. Acquiring a teaching degree in the late fifties and early sixties was a great accomplishment for blacks. For many years, African Americans were deprived of not only going to college but also of going to school, period. When the opportunity presented itself, young blacks took advantage of everything they could.

CHAPTER THREE

WAR, PROTESTS, DEMANDS, AND CHANGES

The mid-60s brought forth a different type of school designed to educate young black men of their heritage and responsibilities. The school was known as the School of Black Awareness. These schools were outreach programs sponsored by the Delta Ministry of Washington County. The young men were eager to learn their heritage and responsibilities as relating to their communities and families. Some of the materials taught came from black history books. The books were written by African American authors—books designed to instill pride and motivation, designed to help young men aspire to be doctors, lawyers, and businessmen. The teachers were men that had a very good vision of the future. There were many lectures by professional people that were invited by members of the Delta Ministry Organization.

The schools were started in few southern states, and they were intended to help build better citizens and neighborhoods. Around the same time, a teen club for recreation also opened. People in the neighborhoods were witnessing the evolution of a different kind of young black man. Some of the senior citizens were not sure of what they were seeing or hearing. The music that young people were listening to was strange and, in some cases, frightening. Special guest speakers would frequently visit the black awareness schools, such as the late great Fannie Lou Hamer and Fred Brown, the brother of H. Rap Brown.

Musical artists like James Brown were saying, "Say It Loud I'm Black and Proud," and, "I Don't Want Nobody to Give Me Nothing, Open Up the Door and I'll Get It Myself." Marvin Gaye was singing, "What's Going On?" There were many other artists writing songs and music relating to the African American experience of their time.

During these days, a most notable change was the war in Southeast Asia (Vietnam). This war was taking young men from all over the country, drafting them by the thousands. Underprivileged young men—white and black—were dying on the front lines of that war every day, along with some Hispanics and Native Americans. There were bodies coming back home by the dozens every month. There were protests all over the country denouncing the war. Many young soldiers were coming home crippled, some were blind, others had PTSD, and others mental problems.

Students in schools all over the country were drafted. This war tested the resolve of this country, but it was never clearly defined. What really was the purpose of sending so many young men over there only to be injured or killed? That question has never truly been answered.

Soon, this war would come close to home. Young men from Greenville were being drafted. Some were drafted in high school when they turned 18 years old while some who had gone off to college were drafted. Many also volunteered to serve in the armed forces.

The war was in the headlines every day of newspapers all over the country. Protests started mounting everywhere, even outside the country, Americans in many neighborhoods had relatives leaving to join the military. Politicians from several states started protesting the war. Nevertheless, the war went on and on, and the President of the United States and Congress seemed to not listen to the cry of the people.

In 1968, Dr. Martin Luther King Jr. was killed in Memphis, Tennessee. His death sparked outrage all over America. He had gone to Memphis to rally with sanitation workers. It was there where he delivered one of his greatest speeches, "I Have Been to the Mountaintop." Dr. King had led the Civil Rights Movement for many years. He had been stabbed and locked in jails. He led marches through the deep south with a nonviolent approach. No matter what he had to endure, Dr. King kept preaching and marching for freedom for his people. He was always up front, marching for equality and justice. He would not stop until the federal government gave in to establish the Civil Rights Act of 1964 for all citizens. These rights gave the African Americans the right to vote; the freedom to enter businesses through the front doors; the freedom to assemble together; the right to live in neighborhoods of choice; the right to attend any public schools in their own neighborhoods, white or black; and the right to attend colleges and universities in America.

Although the Civil Rights Act was passed, it would be many years before the established white culture would comply with the mandates of the federal government. There were many communities around America still segregated and refusing to comply to the government's ruling.

Segregation was deeply embedded into the heart and soul of America. The southern states were defiant against change, with governors fighting against every alteration that the federal government had proposed. They were declaring that individual states should have the right to make laws and decisions, not the federal government.

The schools were their primary concern. They did not want their girls to be exposed to young African American males. They did not want African American teachers laying hands on their children. In order to combat some of these possibilities, all rules of punishment were removed from schools, thus inviting children to become out of control. This same problem exists today in most of these schools. The white children had never attended schools with blacks in Greenville. Fueled by anger, the white students would comply to the teaching of their parents.

In the early days of forced integration, private schools were being built in many southern states. The private schools had tuition fees to keep the poor people—both   black   and   white—from attending. However, there were some not as pricey, but they were white only in the early days. These schools were placed in the heart of white communities. A few blacks were allowed so that the schools could still apply for federal aid grants, better known as "Title One Funds," to school districts that had underprivileged black and white students.

In Greenville, Mississippi, two private schools were built for whites only in 1969. They were Washington School and Greenville Christian. Although both started out predominantly white, these schools could qualify for federal funds from the federal government when some minorities were enrolled. This move by the whites in Greenville diluted the funds that were to be shared by the public schools, leaving the African American public schools, once again, with the bare essentials as they tried to stay open.

After these changes, the black students and teachers were set further back. The African American teachers were paid less than the white teachers and were concerned about retirement benefits, insurance, and pay raises. The black teachers came together to address these many issues and organized a group to deal with them. The teachers established what was known as The ADHOC Committee. Later, they would present them to the school board and the superintendent of the public schools.

The teachers called meetings with the superintendent and the school board to discuss the many issues and demands they had. The meetings were open to the public. Some students heard about the meetings and wanted to sit in on them to see what was actually being said.

The students that attended these meetings were some of the young men that had been brought up in the black awareness schools. These young men were community activists that had concerns about the activities happening in their neighborhoods. Most of these young men attended T.L. Weston Junior/Senior High School, while some were from Coleman High. They were high school students that had been well educated and were very serious about their communities, as it relates to education and economics.

While attending some of these meetings, the students began to notice that the superintendent was very short-spoken with the teachers. At times, he was outright rude. In return, the teachers were often very quiet and soft-spoken. The school board members were in support of the superintendent. The students were very quiet in the meetings, but they became angry when they heard what was said. They had been taught to maintain their "cool" but to take note of everything.

After the third meeting, the students decided to deal with the school administrators on their own terms and organized the other students at both public schools, Coleman and T.L. Weston. The student leaders at each school came together to discuss the issues and concerns that they had. These leaders at both schools were mostly seniors, and nearly all of them had been trained at the black awareness project schools.

CHAPTER FOUR

STUDENTS AND COMMUNITY LEADERS HOLD MEETINGS

In June 1969, community meetings were being held on both sides of Greenville. African Americans were discussing the many issues that they were confronted with all over the city. People from all walks of life would attend the town hall meetings, where talks about boycotting local businesses were frequently brought up and young people were taking active roles in the discussions.

Some ministers in the neighborhoods were conducting similar meetings at their churches. People were meeting in their homes. Change was in the air, and many welcomed the positive meetings. There was a real hope for change in the African American communities.

During these meetings, a few young people were getting noticed for their abilities to speak publicly. They were helping others understand the movement that was taking place in Greenville. Two of these young men were students at T.L. Weston Junior/ Senior High School. They were both good friends growing up and always supported and respected each other. People that knew them had respect for them, teachers and students alike. They were well known in their communities.

These two young men were among those that were attending the meetings with the school board and the teachers. They started to make themselves known throughout the city of Greenville. Frequently attending meetings at city hall to listen to the mayor and the city council discuss city business in the afternoon. They would take notes at the meetings occasionally. They did not say anything, they were not there to protest—only to observe what was being said.

Neither the mayor nor the council would openly object to them attending the meetings. The meetings were open to the public. The young men conducted themselves like well-mannered young men, although they appeared to be a group of concerned young blacks. After listening to the city council, the group would discuss what the council had addressed. They started taking an active part in community issues. Young black people were learning how the system worked, which was the goal of the Delta Ministry Program.

The time had finally come for the students at T.L. Weston and Coleman to make a list of their own demands. Some of the demands were (1) new updated textbooks, (2) Black History in high school,

(3) updated science department materials, (4) better food in the cafeteria, and (5) new updated equipment in athletic and musical departments. The major demand from the students at Weston was for their principal to resign). These demands were meant to improve their respective schools. Soon, the students would have opportunity to present them to the superintendent and the school board.

In September of 1969, school started again in Greenville. T.L. Weston Junior/Senior High School had been rated excellent in sports and music in the state over the past five years. The students that began their education at T.L. Weston in the seventh grade were now seniors, and many of them had been involved in making their school well-known inside and outside the state of Mississippi. In sports, they were very hard to beat. The choir was very good. The school had moved from the Little Six Conference to the Big Eight Conference. The football team had dominated the Little Six Conference with three championship titles with only four games lost in five years. In one of the football games the team scored the state record of 103 points. The basketball team was bidding for their second conference championship. The concert band had been rated excellent in the state two years back to back. The athletic programs were among the top in the state, and the students had earned many academic achievements and awards. This senior class was a very tight group; they had become a family. This senior class was one of a kind.

Looming large in the minds of these students was the fact that for eleven long years, they had to deal with handed-down books, used equipment, outdated material, bad food, and a principal that lived in the past. Complaints from students were not allowed no matter what the problems were. The principal just did not help the situation at all. He treated the students and teachers unfair by talking to them very rude most of the time. He yelled instead of talking calm, using scare tactics.

Some of the older students were meeting off campus to discuss ways they could have their voices heard. Student leaders were actively involved in many of the community meetings. The time had come to challenge the "separate but equal" education system. The leaders had total respect and trust of the student body. All of the senior athletes were with them, including the entire football team. Some of the young men in the lower classes were ready and willing to do what they were asked to do. The students came up with a plan to seize the school in protest to make sure that their voices were heard.

The student body leaders from T.L. Weston called the student body leaders from Coleman to make plans to seize both high schools the morning of September 23, 1969, at 7:30 a.m. They were depending on the element of surprise. The plan was to get to school early to take control of all entryways and exits of the schools. All students would be directed to the auditoriums. There, they would assemble together to have their voices heard on their terms, not the administrators' terms.

In addition to the plan to assemble in the auditoriums, curriers would go from one school to the other to ensure that the plans were being carried out. Their number-one concern was to protect the younger children in the lower grades. In case of trouble, the students were to stand down and not cause any type of violent act. Their goal was to have a peaceful protest, without violence. The leaders talked to the street gangs and young people that were known dropouts in the communities. By talking to those guys, they could carry out this well-planned event to make sure that there was no outside interference on their part.

Student Cacus Meet No Trouble

CHAPTER FIVE

THE STUDENTS TAKE CONTROL OF THE AUDITORIUM

As the students of T.L. Weston Junior/Senior High School arrived for school on the morning of September 23, 1969, the leaders were standing at the entry ways and exits to the school buildings, and they were successful in sending all of the students that showed up for school to the auditorium. The students moved quietly and quickly to get to seats in the auditorium. The teachers were shocked; they had no idea what was going on. The leaders were on stage hooking up the mics. They started to greet the students, explaining what was about to take place. The auditorium was filling up with over seven hundred students. Everyone seemed to be ok after the leaders informed them why they were there and that they would stay there all day and night if they had to. The teachers began to peep into the auditorium, but they would not enter. The assistant principal, who was also the head football coach, was trying to talk to some of the senior football players in the hallway, but they ignored him then joined the other students in the auditorium.

When the principal of the school saw what was going on, he immediately called the police and the superintendent of the public schools. The leaders continued to address the students, and the principal was overwhelmed and shocked. He realized that he was out of control as T.L. Weston had fallen into the hands of the students. He was yelling at the student body president, telling him to get off the mic and commanding the students to get to their classrooms. He was wasting his time and breath; the students were telling him to shut up and to go to his office. Some of the senior girls and boys were acting as ushers. The leaders were continuing to inform the student body about the cause and purpose of not going to class.

The students wanted a change to take place, and they were going to ensure that it happened.

The south end students had shown that they had grit, and they had learned how to stay together under most circumstances and conditions. These students came from very low-income homes. Their parents worked long hours for very little pay, and they had to grow up fast. During the summers when school was out, many of them worked in the cotton fields. They were tough, to say the least.

After the students had been in the auditorium for over an hour, the superintendent showed up with the entire Greenville police force. The school was surrounded by police and the local sheriff's department. The state highway troopers were stationed along the highway about a quarter mile from the school. T.L. Weston was surrounded. The superintendent came on the stage where the leaders were gathered. He was yelling, "Go to class or get out of the building!" "Get out!" Reporters from the local newspaper, The Delta Democrat Times, showed up. They started writing the story as it unfolded. The superintendent told a black police officer to clear the stage. The officer charged the student body president, causing him to jump off the stage, which was about five feet high. The students started throwing books at the superintendent and the police.

After the superintendent told the students to go to class or leave the school, the leaders had the students exit the building and proceed to the school grounds. Once outside of the school and onto the grounds near the front entrance, the leaders asked the students to line up according to their grade level. They started with the seventh-grade students first, following the seventh graders the eighth graders, then the ninth graders, and on and on until all of the junior high students were in line. After that the tenth graders and all of the junior and senior girls were in line, the senior and junior boys surrounded the entire group. The students left the school and walked to Maud Bryant Park.

When the students arrived at Maud Bryant Park, they all gathered around to listen to the leaders of the student body give directions regarding the next course of action to take. Someone in the crowd started yelling, "Tear the books up, tear the books up!" The students had been complaining for years about the used, handed-down books from the white schools. All of the students yelled, "Tear the books up, tear the books up!" They began tearing up all books that they had with them. When they finished, torn-up books were piled up over two feet high and thirty feet wide. There were eight hundred students at that park with some parents and members of the communities. The students had made a historic move. Back then, parents knew what the students wanted; they knew that the black schools were not treated right. All of the parents at that park were backing their children because they knew that the children were very serious. The students had started a fire that would be hard to put out. The students were well organized, and they were staging a nonviolent protest like never seen before in the state of Mississippi. The students had caught the administrators completely by surprise. The law enforcement agencies were waiting to arrest the leaders, but they too were surprised to see how well organized the protest was carried out. The students did nothing to provoke the law enforcers except destroy the books.

The people in the community heard about what the children had done at the school. They were lining the streets in the neighborhood, going to the park to see what the children were doing. The police were present, but they stayed back, trying not to pose a threat. The deputy sheriffs and the state troopers had moved back to let the city police monitor the park.

Before the crowd left the park, the leaders told the students, "All of us are going to school tomorrow morning. Everyone should go to the auditorium when you get to school. Tomorrow, we will present our demands." The leaders urged the students to go straight home and not to wander around in the neighborhood. "Look out for the police and don't say anything to them," they told the group. "All of us need to be at the school around the same time," one of the students said to the leaders. The leader said, "We need to stay together; therefore, we will be stronger together."

While the students were in the park, two of the seniors had the responsibility to drive across town to check on Coleman High School. When they returned from Coleman, they had news that the Coleman students were not successful; they all were convinced to go to their classes. After hearing the news from Coleman, the leaders at Weston were really disappointed. They all had planned together with the belief that if both schools were able to be shut down at the same time, the school board and the superintendent would have to give in to their demands. Thus the first day of the protest ended with the job half done, according to the leaders. The T.L. Weston students went home after walking out of the school together.

Later that evening, the television news channels all across the state of Mississippi were reporting on the protest at T.L. Weston. Since the TV stations were not on the scene, they relied on the Delta Democrat Newspaper for their information. The people of Greenville were glued the television watching and reading the report in the local newspaper. The students had made headline news all over the state and beyond. People in the communities, both black and white, were surprised by the manner the students conducted themselves. They had never witnessed students being so bold and disciplined, especially African American students. The leaders had planned a movement that would be talked about for years to come. It was evident that they children had taken a page out of Dr. Martin Luther King Jr.'s nonviolent approach to pull this off; otherwise, their walkout may have had a complete different outcome.

The following day, September 24, 1969, the students arrived at school and headed straight to the auditorium. The student body president greeted the students, parents, teachers, and members of the Delta Ministry. He talked about the list of demands that had been discussed at the school board meeting held the night before, where the teachers and the board discussed the demands presented by the students and the teachers. The students and the parents were all paying close attention to what was being said. The leader of the teachers' delegation was a man known in the community for working for changes in all of the public schools where African Americans attended. He reminded the school board that a boycott of the businesses was hanging in the balance if all of the demands weren't met.

The actions of the students at T.L. Weston gave momentum to the ongoing protest that the teachers had started. The students' walkout all but sealed the deal. The students caught mostly everyone by surprise, except the leader of the teachers' delegates. He was one of the teachers that taught the Black Awareness Project. The student leaders knew him and trusted him; he was one of their mentors for many years. On the night before the walkout, the student leaders from both schools were at his home, discussing the plans for the next morning.

After the meeting with the board, the white teachers had a closed meeting to discuss the situation confronting the board. The business owners also were involved in the process. They did not want or need a boycott to take place in Greenville. The students had impacted and created a concern like never before in the city. Not only Greenville, but the governor and lawmakers weighed in on the students' protest. The businesses in that city were targeted for protest. After two hours in the auditorium, the students returned to their classrooms, with the exception of the senior and junior boys that attended the vocation center. The student body president asked them to stay at the school and not to travel by bus to the vocation center until all demands had been met and the protest was completed. His reason for asking them not to leave the school was that he wanted them to be the security force to protect the other students, to monitor the halls, and to keep the peace. The principal had backed off the students, who had asked for his resignation.

The students left the auditorium going to their classes. They met some of the seniors from Coleman High School walking in the direction of the auditorium. The students from Coleman stopped to talk to the senior leaders. The Coleman students had come to support the students at T.L. Weston, and they were highly disappointed that they did not follow through with the plans. Some of those students were family and good friends. There was nothing negative said in the exchange between the students, and although they were crosstown rivals, the students had great respect for one another. The Coleman High football team beat Weston in their first game. Coleman was a powerhouse in the Big Eight Conference, and

T.L. Weston had recently joined The Big Eight Conference.

On September 25, 1969, the students met in the auditorium for the third morning. The student body president addressed the audience, calling for a boycott if the demands were not met. He said if the answer to the demands was "no," they would start the boycott on Monday, but if the answer was "yes," then things would go back to normal. The students had their agendas, and they did not trust all of the teachers.

One of the teacher leaders told the audience that the only answer that would be accepted was "yes." She said that the teachers were confident about the outcome of meeting. She served as the sponsor for the student government at T.L. Weston also senior advisor. The students trusted her. There were parents in the auditorium for the third day, supporting and watching the students. People from the neighborhood were there as well. The students were leading the protest.

The student body president announced that there would be a meeting at one of the lodges on the north side at nine that night. The meeting was called to hear results of the vote from the school board and the business owners concerning the demands. He encouraged all of the people in the auditorium to attend the meeting. (Delta Democrat Times 9/25/1969) p1

CHAPTER SIX

THE DEMANDS ARE PENDING

On Wednesday night September 25, 1969, the school board, the superintendent, white teachers committee, and business owners voted yes to accept the demands that had been presented to them by the student body at T.L. Weston Junior/Senior High School and the teachers' committee. This vote opened the door for change in Greenville, Mississippi. Finally, the small door of opportunity had opened. After over five years since the passing of the Civil Rights Act, Greenville, Mississippi decided to comply with the federal mandate.

When the decision of the vote got to the African Americans at the lodge, there were sighs of relief from the leaders of both groups and the residents of the community. The people of Greenville had been watching the protest. There was some outside interference from hate groups, but they were not going to stop the movement. The African American people of Greenville were standing up together for the same cause—protesting for their children to get a good education. The list of demands would ensure that the city's public schools would help the teachers to get better pay, insurance, and working conditions. As for the students, major changes needed to happen—new books, African American history courses, better and new equipment for all departments, better food in the cafeteria. Last but not least, the principal retired.

A few weeks after the protest, there were some improvements. New books were replacing old ones, especially the books that were destroyed at the park. The football team got two new sets of uniforms. The both the girls' and boys' basketball teams got new uniforms as well. The food in the cafeteria had improved, and new supplies were being purchased for the labs. The teachers seemed happy about their jobs. The black history course was even offered to the seniors first. All seemed to be well.

Before the end of the first semester, a decision had been made by the Mississippi Board of Education to integrate all schools the following year. This sudden decision had a lot of people, especially the high school students, really concerned. Their greatest concern was where they would attend school the next year. Students that were juniors would be seniors the following school year, and they soon learned that all public high school juniors and seniors would be attending Greenville High School, a school where only whites had been attending. T.L. Weston Junior/Senior High School would become a school for tenth grade students only.

Greenville High School was located on the east central side of the city. A citywide bus route was put in place for the next school year to accommodate the new plan. Coleman High School was to be converted to a junior high school. Teachers received new assignments that would cause them to be moved all over the city.

After the signing of the Civil Rights Act, all states were given time to prepare for the changes that were to come. Mississippi and other southern states were continuing to build private schools for the white students in order to segregate them from people of color.

The students at T.L. Weston had done what no one in the history of the state of Mississippi had ever done: they had staged a nonviolent protest to bring about real change for education in Mississippi.

Weston Students Meet Again

CHAPTER SEVEN

A COMPLETE CHANGE IN DIRECTIONS FOR THE PEOPLE OF GREENVILLE

The citizens of Greenville were dealing with a changing time. The white students at Greenville High School who could afford to were preparing to attend Washington School, and others planned to transfer to St. Joseph School or stay at Greenville High School. The African Americans did not have much choice. The children of doctors, lawyers, some teachers, and business owners could afford to send their kids to private school. Some parents held common labor jobs.

The future was very cloudy for the people of Greenville. After many years of segregation, the city was all but forced to obey the law. The African Americans were concerned about the white teachers mistreating their children. The black women were especially concerned because they helped raise many of those white people, and they did not trust many of those white people. Some of the white parents were too busy doing other things so they allowed black women to help raise their children, and the black women listened to many conversations between the white parents and their children. Black women were very concerned about their children.

From the pulpits of only a few churches, pastors were bold enough the speak the truth to their congregations. On Sundays at those few churches, these pastors warned the parents and children. Often, they would tell the children to take advantage of the opportunity to learn all that they could. The pastors would tell them to always keep God first in whatever they did.

In the spring of 1970, the first seventh grade class that walked into T.L. Weston in 1964 was ready to graduate in May. They had been there for six years. The leaders of this class and the other seniors had made history at T.L. Weston. They would leave a legacy that would be known for decades to come. This class graduated more than ten honor students. Many of them were offered scholarships. They were leaving as championships in football, basketball, baseball, track and field, music, and art. Many of them went off to college. The students in the Class of 1970 will always be remembered for their leadership and their nonviolent Protest that helped to change the educational system in the state of Mississippi.

After graduating from high school, some of the young people moved north to the larger cities in Illinois, Missouri, Indiana, Michigan, New York, and some moved west to Texas and California. There were a few jobs in Greenville that paid decent wages, but these jobs were given mostly to the white citizens, leaving very little choice to young African Americans. Many of them had relatives that had moved away to northern states to find good jobs, and some of them found very good paying jobs. Young black people did not want to stay in Mississippi.

At the start of the fall semester in 1970, the first African American seniors and juniors stepped foot in Greenville High School. As referenced by some of the students that were in those classes, the whites were intentionally separated from the blacks. After the black kids saw what was happening, they banded together. Some had been the heart of the walkout at T.L. Weston, and they were ready to take on whatever was coming their way. The African American students were very strong and bold. They resisted any bad treatment that came their way. The white teachers were not going to get away with treating those students with no respect. The black kids in Greenville had been living in the storm most of their lives, so they understood hard times.

However, with a rough start, both sides were divided, even in the classrooms. This continued for a while until time brought about changes. The students eventually began to interact with each other. They soon realized that they had only a short time to be at Greenville High School.

The students that attended junior high schools did not take long before they would learn to get along. The tenth-grade students were bussed from all over the city to attend T.L. Weston. While they were at Weston, they played sports with the students at Greenville High School. Many of the tenth-grade students felt so out of place, having to ride the buses from school to school.

According to a massive federal survey of US educational inequality, if desegregation were to work anywhere in the Deep South, it would be Greenville. This city was called an oasis of tolerance and pragmatic gentility in the Mississippi Delta, the blackest, poorest, most southern place on earth. Greenville was to be the beacon of hope for integration.

The Coleman Report became legendary; it started debates that are still alive today. But there's nothing in the publication's account that reveals that the city was Greenville, Mississippi, since the name remained anonymous. There was no tracking system in place to see if its promise came true. Did the integration plan succeed in bringing a deeply divided community together to improve education for both black and white students?

The town of Greenville was an unusually diverse community of blacks, whites, Chinese, Creoles, and Jews, as well as immigrants from Lebanon and Syria. Home to more than twelve thousand public school children, the district was the first in Mississippi to defy the government by voluntarily offering a real choice for white and black children to enroll in each other's schools.

Although Greenville managed to integrate the city's schools, there were minor problems. However, some Mississippi towns had serious problems. In Grenada, Mississippi, angry white residents beat black elementary children with pipes and fists for trying to enroll in that town's token "freedom of choice plan."

In Yazoo City, Mississippi, the White City Council strong-armed fifty-three black citizens for signing an NAACP petition endorsing integrated schools. Some of the blacks were fired from their jobs, others were evicted from their homes, and all were refused service at the town's white-owned grocery stores. (The Nation 10/13/2016) p1

CHAPTER EIGHT

PAST DECISIONS AND CYNICAL VIEWS FOUNDED THE TOWN'S EARLY SYSTEMS

The US Civil Rights Commission declared Greenville's desegregation to be a success, not just in deeds but also in hearts and minds. According to the commission, "Good leadership and good will had created a district where not one school is left with an all-black student body." However, during this time about two thousand white students had enrolled in Washington Private School or St. Joseph High School or had moved out of Greenville.

Greenville caught the attention of the Coleman Report researchers in 1965 when its school board defied Mississippi segregationist governor, Paul B. Johnson Jr., and the obstructionist white citizens' councils to submit its own choice of plan to the US Department of Education.

Commissioned by the Civil Rights Act to study the state of school inequality across the United States, the nation's top sociologist, James Coleman, undertook a massive survey of around six hundred thousand students in a little over a year's time. In the 749-page report, officially called Equality of Educational Opportunity, Coleman expected to find that vast discrepancies in resources in schools with concentrated racial isolation and poverty was crucial, but they did not make a big dent in children's achievement. What did matter was integration.

As an incentive to integrate, the federal government offered emergency dollars to districts whose desegregation plans were approved. As disincentive, it threatened to withhold new Title One funds for disadvantaged students from districts that refused to comply. According to the Hechinger News Report, Greenville, like many other towns in Mississippi, established two school systems by the late 19th century, which were segregated by race and wholly unequal in money, facilities, and trained teachers from the offset.

Hodding Carter Jr., the founder of Greenville's Delta Democrat Times and winner of the Pulitzer Prize, had little quarrel with the idea of dual school systems but condemned their inequality. He blamed the entire state for bringing on the Brown v. Board of Education decision in 1954. If ever a region asked for such a decision, the south did through its shocking, calculated, and cynical disobedience to its own state's constitution, which said school systems must be equal, he wrote at the time: "For seventy-five years, we sent negro kids to school in hovels and pig pens."

CHAPTER NINE

EFFECTS OF DESEGREGATION IN GREENVILLE

Finally, black and white children and teachers were fully integrated class by class and school by school. Town leaders put to use nearly every integration tool available to ensure a fair mix of students and teachers. Elementary school populations were also merged. T.L. Weston became a tenth-grade school, and Greenville High admitted all the town's juniors and seniors. Black and white teachers were evenly distributed, zoning laws were changed, and curriculums were altered. Black History was added, and busing was provided. There was a real effort to make integration work.

In the early beginnings, the city of Greenville, Mississippi seemed determined to give integration a chance to be successful. It would be up to the administrators, teachers, parents, and students to comply. The story would be told in a few years to come. Time was a very important factor for the people of Greenville to reject or accept the new way of life as their children were going to school in the new public school system.

For the first time, Greenville schools had a busing system. The children no longer had to walk to school. The buses carried the students to their schools every day. Some of the students that lived close to their schools chose to walk unless bad weather occurred. The newly acquired bus systems opened jobs for blacks that had commercial driver's licenses and good driving records. Things were seemly looking up for the Greenville communities.

In the mid-70s, the number of white students that were enrolled in the town's schools began to drop quickly. The parents of the white students were moving out of Greenville. A greater percent of white students began enrolling into Washington Academy private school. The rate of the white students leaving caused concern by black civil rights leaders in Greenville. The public schools were funded by the number of students enrolled and attending classes.

According to some African American students that were attending Greenville High School in the mid-70s, the white students were leaving so fast that the school appeared to become all black. The junior high schools were having the same issues with the white students leaving. The flight of white students in Greenville started about five years into the integration. Their absence from the public school program caused great concern among blacks. The leaders of the African American community started to believe this was a well- thought-out plan by the white community leaders. As far as they were concerned, the fate of the public school system was slowly being handed over to the African Americans.

From the very start, the Coleman Report was only guessing when it came to Greenville. As a city that was supposed to be the ideal place to desegregate a population—based on diversity among the races—Greenville was turning out to be a bad idea. The white people of Greenville and many other Mississippi towns refused to accept forced integration.

Still, the whites continued to control the distribution of funds allocated to Greenville. Many of the black leaders questioned the flow of money to the private schools in the city. The blacks had very little knowledge of the amount of money that was allocated to the town each year.

CHAPTER TEN

THE FAILURE OF DESEGREGATION AND INTEGRATION IN GREENVILLE

The Hechinger News reported Bob Boyd remembers the day he believes the great promise of Greenville was upended. Boyd, a lifelong Mississippi civil-rights worker, had landed his first job after he graduated from Ole Miss in 1968. He worked as a news and court reporter for the Delta Democrat Times. His editor, Hodding Carter III, was informed of a secret meeting scheduled to be held at the Buster Brown Community Center located across from Greenville High School. Mr. Boyd was sent to cover the secret meeting, which occurred several days after a federal court had decided in favor of the black plaintiffs who had pressed for a speedier desegregation in 1969. Some in the white communities were upset at such interference.

Boyd was not an invited guest at this secret meeting that was scheduled for the white community leaders; therefore, he had to stay clear and not bring attention to himself. He peeped through the door of the center long enough to see that it was packed to capacity. Once those in the meeting noticed that he was standing at the doors, knowing that he was a reporter, they asked him to leave the building. Boyd recalled seeing around two hundred white citizens from the community's meeting to discuss opening Washington High School, the newly built private high school for white students.

Mr. Boyd expresses his belief that the story of Greenville would have been different if Washington School had never opened. The black leaders in the community believed that the school gave the white students a means of escaping integration. Many blamed the deceit of the school board, business owners, and white parents for the fall of the public school system in Greenville, Mississippi. (The Nation 10/13/2016 p1)

Several factories and other businesses began moving away from Greenville around the end of the 70s. With the closing of factories and businesses, other problems were also developing in Greenville. The once great port city was being deserted due to forced integration. Some of the towboat companies were moving upriver around Memphis. People that worked for some of the companies, could keep their jobs if they were willing to relocate.

Both white and black students that were graduating from high school were either going off to college, moving north or west, joining the armed forces, or leaving Greenville, Mississippi and not returning. The few white students that remained in public school were those who simply could not afford to pay tuition at the private academy schools.

Greenville was once known as the chosen city to spearhead the desegregation agenda brought by The Civil Rights Commission of the federal government. Greenville was falling very hard. The fall was felt throughout the city in all areas of life. The citizens of Greenville that controlled the bulk of the wealth were leaving and refusing to support the future growth of the city. It soon became very clear to the African American community that the city was being abandoned by the white citizens. The blacks were dealing with this situation without having any power to do anything. Meanwhile, the African American students continued to go to school. The black children were brought up in a racially-divided city, where they learned to make the best of a bad situation.

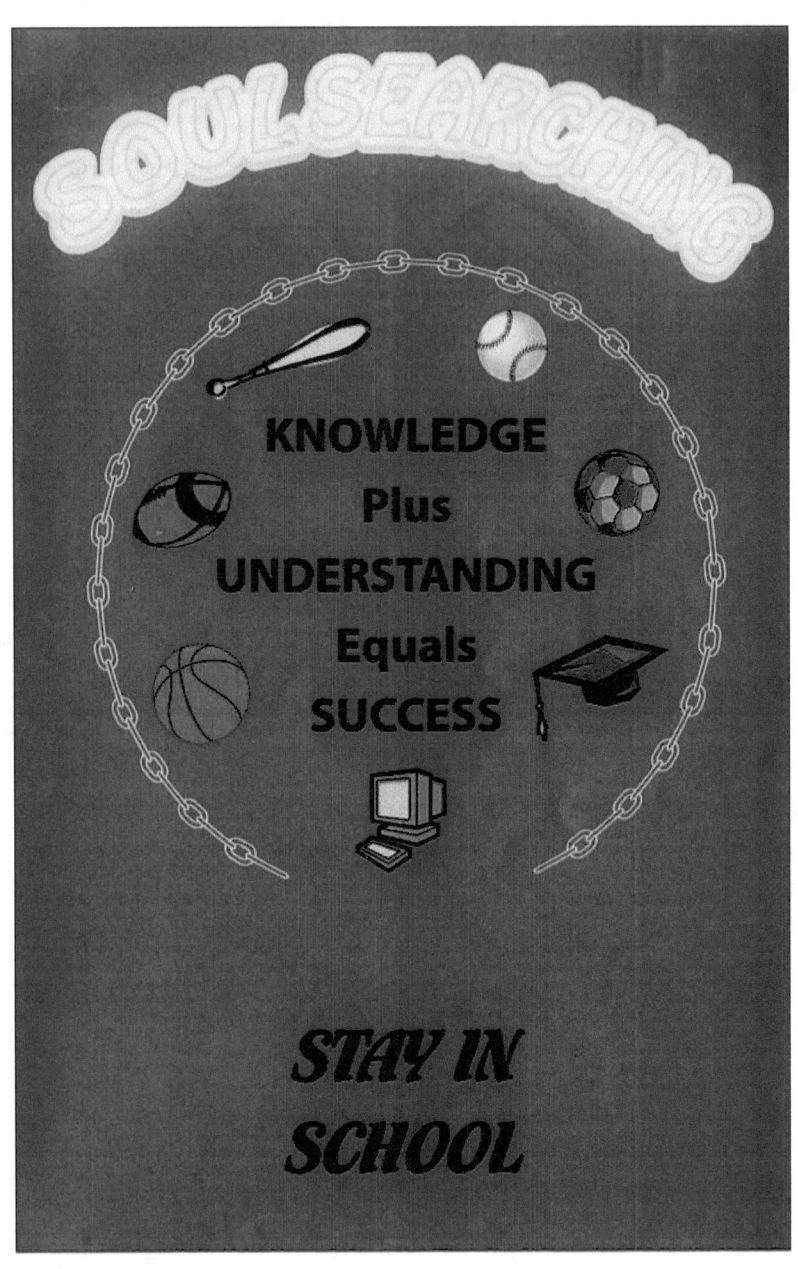

Knowledge Plus Understanding Equal Success

CHAPTER ELEVEN

GREENVILLE'S PUBLIC SCHOOLS FIGHT TO STAY OPEN

Many years have passed, and the city of Greenville has been all but abandoned by the white population. In the late 70s, the population was around sixty thousand citizens. The current population is 31,500. The schools that were converted due to desegregation have decreased, yet the city is still functional. Over the years, the city has been short-changed by the Mississippi state legislature. The public schools have become grossly underfunded. The leadership in the public school system has been lackluster when it comes to setting high standards for the students.

The African American people must continue to stride forward. Years ago in Greenville, African Americans stood up for equality and change. The African American people of Greenville protested and fought for education for their children. The survival of the public school system is very important. In the old days, the challenges were far greater. The parents and teachers worked together. The teachers respected the parents, and the parents respected the teachers.

Back in the day, African Americans in the communities pulled together. They were praying and hoping that their children could have a better life. Some believe that if the pioneers of the old days were here today, Greenville would be far better off than its current condition. As long as there is one person looking for a change, then hope is alive.

Maybe someday this city, which was once known as the Great River City will shine its bright lights again. This will happen only if the citizens of this once great city work together. The economic survival of the city of Greenville greatly depends on sound leadership. Incoming businesses that will provide good jobs. Jobs that will attract young people to stay home to help grow the economy.

After sharing this information in Walkout, I pray for future generations. I pray that something written in this book will give understanding to what education meant to students of the 60s and 70s. The African American students of that time showed a zeal and thirst for education. Having to deal with many obstacles as mentioned in this book, the students confronted inequalities, racism, outdated equipment, and limited resources. Through it all, the students of yesterday set a standard with their nonviolent protest to gain a voice to help improve the quality of education that present generations have full access to.

Today in Greenville, the African American students are confronted with a different but almost identical set of issues. At the highest level of these issues is safety in a segregated society, marked by unequal sharing of funds for public schools. However, with modern technology and advanced curricular information, today's school systems are far better than yesterday's. Education is the key to opening closed doors, but the students must take advantage of the moment to advance and prosper. Education is vital in today's world. To God Be the Glory.

Cotton Fields

One day we crossed the sea in shame
Tied to each other -- who's to blame
Made to work all day for free
Go to sleep tired as can be

Daylight comes very soon
Sun gets hot just before noon
Cotton rows very long
Might as well sing a song

Sing all day - don't worry about pay
The lord is watching everything
Why do people act so mean?
Cotton getting very tall
I'll be working in the gin this fall

A snake is lying in the middle of the row
Big mama killed him with a hoe
The people are praying for a breeze
Nothing but cotton - there are no trees
The dirt under my feet is very hot
I'm looking for a shady spot
The boss is looking at the ground
The children are chopping the cotton down
He yells with a loud voice to the crowd
Send the kids to the bus
I see no one is feeling proud
Then he began to cuss

Everyone heard what he said
No one out here is afraid
Big mama said boy - let's go
Down we went - down the cotton row

AUTOBIOGRAPHY

My name is Arthur Lee Brown, author of WALKOUT. Born February 18, 1952. My parents were Minister William Brown and Clara Brown, who are now both deceased. My birthplace is Chatham, Mississippi, twenty miles south of Greenville, Mississippi. My parents moved to Greenville when I was three years old. I finished high school in the spring of 1970. Joined the United States Air Force March 4, 1971. After my 4 year obligation to service I received an honorable discharge August 6 1974 with the rank of Sargent. Later I received a certificate of Ordination from the Baptist Church November 1997. I founded the Christian Youths United Online Outreach Ministry http://www.christianyouthsunited.com in October 2012. I am the father of 3 daughters, 6 grandchildren and 1 great grand. In this Book I am the Student Body President.

NOTES

1. Lynell Hancock, "The Anonymous Town That Was the Model of Desegregation In the Civil-Rights Era" "The Coleman Report Researchers Federal Survey" "Early Mississippi School Systems" The Nation News Paper, October 3, 2016 p1

2. Hodding Carter Jr. "Weston Pupils Halt Morning Classes" "Student Caucus at Weston No Trouble" "Weston Students Meet Again" Delta Democrat Times News Paper September 23-25 1969 p1

BIBLIOGRAPHY

Hancock, Lynell. October 3, 2016. The H.Gordon Garbedian Professor of Journalism and Director of Spencer Fellowship Program at the Columbia Journalism School. "The anonymous Town that was the Model of Desegregation in the Civil-Rights Era," Voluntary desegregation Freedom of Choice, (Hechinger News Report) 475 Riverside Drive suite 650, New York, NY 10115

Coleman, Robert. 1965. Sociologist, Coleman Report Researchers Federal Survey of US educational inequalities, (Greenville was singled out as a beacon of hope for school integration in the South according to the authors of the landmark civil rights era Coleman Report) Commissioned by the 1964 Civil Rights ACT, 1331 Pennsylvania Avenue NW Suite 1150 Washington, DC 20425.

Carter, Hoddin Jr, (Pulitzer Prize Winner) (Founder), Carter, Hoddin

III Chief Editor, Bob Boyd Reporter, (1888, 1968, 1969). Weston Pupils Hault Morning Classes, Students Caucus at Weston No Trouble, Weston Students Meet Again, Early Mississippi School Systems, 988 North Broadway, PO Box 1618 Greenville, Mississippi 38701. (Delta Democrat Times News) Catherine, Kirk News Editor.

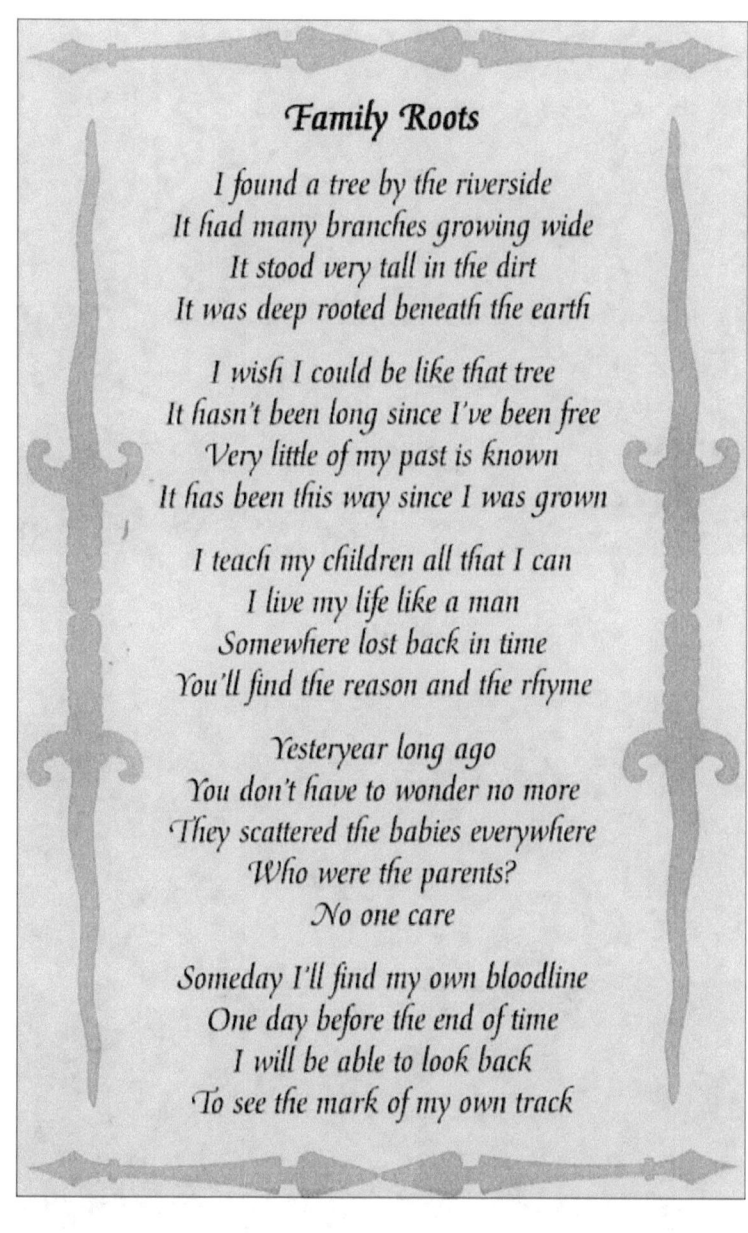

Family Roots

I found a tree by the riverside
It had many branches growing wide
It stood very tall in the dirt
It was deep rooted beneath the earth

I wish I could be like that tree
It hasn't been long since I've been free
Very little of my past is known
It has been this way since I was grown

I teach my children all that I can
I live my life like a man
Somewhere lost back in time
You'll find the reason and the rhyme

Yesteryear long ago
You don't have to wonder no more
They scattered the babies everywhere
Who were the parents?
No one care

Someday I'll find my own bloodline
One day before the end of time
I will be able to look back
To see the mark of my own track

Family Roots

Watermelons

Purple Hull Peas